Surrender to Seduction

by

Socrateez

Heathens House Publishing
Houston

Printed in the United States of America

Surrender to Seduction
ISBN: 1930112319

Enchanted Muze Publishing
www.HeathensHouse.com

Cover Design and Photography:

Elton McWashington
emc2artwork.com

10   9   8   7   6   5   4   3   2   1

This book is dedicated to
Avery Thomas
the son time would not allow me to know

Contents

Surrender

rainy days and innocent nights

are the best moments to let our

love take flight

with soft melodies and scented delights,

we are at liberty to feel

our lust's eminent plight

an ease of emotion and a gentle breeze of light ...

allows this juncture to be known

that there is nothing

more right

And

And there you were,
resting in the bosom of a bed
that embraced your every move …
that enhanced your every thought …
that engulfs you like I wish to

And like prey, you were
attentive to the motions of your aggressor …
the illusiveness of interrogation …
the cunning by candlelight …
the progressions of passivity

And in the time it takes for Destiny to
detour Desire, you moved me
Ringing in my ears like a melodic
overture that debuts before a king,
you moved me
Appealing to my eyes like a blind man from
birth who sees the sun for the first time,
you moved me

And if these things you do to me before
we even begin to see,
then curse the sun ... moon ... and stars
I want you to take me to another
galaxy

And like
Ying and Yang,
we need to be
What is the aromatic essence of
pleasure embraced,
if I cannot embrace you?
It is as useless as ...
as a kingdom with no king ...
as a song with no notes ...
as a kiss with no passion

And let there be more to
life, than mere living
Let there be two streams that
flow to one sea
Let there be treasures
found in the valley of
you and me
Let there be light in
obscurity

And like rain, we are held by
a thought from heaven ...
only to fall in union with nature ...
where we soak in our submissions ...
where we pacify our passions ...
where we drown in our desires
only to be caught up in
rapture and start again

And there you were ...

Battle Hymn

That's when change takes place …

when you are able to

Finally come to terms with

the trials you have faced!

Noting your losses and counting your tears …

it's never easy to accept

your shortcomings …

but add the time and count the years!

How long shall the pain last?

Interesting how we analyze the

Future, criticize the present

and yet live in the past!

Certainty is an illusion … a mere mirage

Get around the detour

Climb over the mountain

Break down the barrage!

Get up … stand up … it is your life

Anything worth having requires a

struggle

Struggle, warrants opposition, but

be strong and remember why you fight!

Victory awaits you … don't you know?

Winners are defined by

completion,

not how fast or slow!

Hold on

Be strong

The line is up ahead!!!

the Blue flame

It is a power
I cannot deny
Your eyes so entrapping,
I will not try
There are so many things
I want to show you
can I?
Bare
I stand before you
I dare you to join me
Naked, I wish to share the
joy of fire
Have you ever
danced in the blue flame?
As I caress your
mind, your body will
never be the same
Ignited by a kiss
and
fed by passion,
this Lambada has no

lead
Hold me and do as you please,
pleasure is for the taking
Tonight ...
yours will I seize

Naked I kneel at your
feet
Prostrating at the
beauty before me
Allow me to kiss
them,
as a token of my tribute
Do not move
Just stand there
and receive
gentle submissions of
my passion
I want to climb your trees,
so that I may play in your forest
Inhaling the essence you emit,
am I wrong in wanting to stay here?
If passion is truly your pleasure, then
let me please you past persecution
Let's dance in the
blue flame
Let's partake in the

heart of the fire
With you, I am more than
incited ... it seems I sear
Desire has cast her
spell
I hold the flame in my
hand and ask you
can the flame be
entrusted to you?
Will you care for it?
How shall it be passed on?
A mere kiss?
Let me slowly set your
forest aflame
not to destroy it, but
to purge it
Can you feel the fire?
Do you feel it swelling inside you?
Traveling to the center
of your sanctuary,
I see I have a home

Don't be vexed about the inferno,
concentrate on the heat
Let it distend inside you
I worry not about the
fire

Why does a mother worry
for her child, if not that
it receives food, security, and love?
Let us feed this flame
Let us ensure the intensity of its power
Let us love this union that no longer separates us

We are now
one
I dare not try to abandon you
For my flame has found a
home
Let me hold you, so that
we may burn together
in the heart of the fire

Cannon of the Cursed

I feel so out of place ...

like a lake in the Sahara,

something seems so very wrong

Enchanted with ignorance,

my mind is plagued with poverty

Longing for simplicities, yet

creating complexities

Even Beauty is seized by the

horror of a putrid end

The realization that my greatest

Fear is my fortune

Loneliness, so it seems, is

my pleasure ...

my pain ...

my curse

But, to what end?

Convenience?

Contempt?

Or am I just contrary?

Kneeling in deep contrition,

I can't help but notice ...

I am alone

I am out of place

I am a lake in the Sahara

Strange ...

what is the expectancy of

a lake in the Sahara?

Complete Me

I sat at my desk watching the rain fall from a window
I had not dare try in at least a decade

My memories descend on ascended thoughts that
lead me to question moves I have made with
the lessers
...
those that did not deserve my greatness
not that they received fakeness
but just were not afforded the fullness
position players who read the requirements
and rocked their roles
came candidly in as if time was supposed to stop
when they found it fitting to award me with a slice of
their pumpkin pie
when I
warrant the spoon, the pan, the left over batter ...
and well yeah, the mixing bowl
the mixer, the hourglass, heat in the oven and space
to remix and sit the edible wet dream on the stove
...

ever notice that position players don't help mate a
home,
yet bend over backwards so that they may fulfill your
fantasies?
However, when you seek to promote position players
to permanent status, you often find yourself standing
in the shadows of Insanity

and I smiled
the rain continued to fall fulfilling it's purpose
and I aim reminded of mine
and I smiled
the wind shook the arms of trees removing dead
leaves
and I began to remove mine
and I smiled
because natural is the fitting conclusion to this order
of things
as is the conclusion of mine
and just as I figure my smile cannot get any larger,
I am reminded of just how much you compliment me
…
and my smile gets just a
touch of love lifted harder

That radiant glow I had dreamed of having as a child
has finally been found

You make my soul sing without ever uttering a word

...

and truth be told, my dear, you honestly do not have
to be around
Thinking on how simple love truly should be
and how hard the lessers have made things seem ...
is it ever really irrational to question that you are not
a dream?

I must apologize because I mentally murdered Judas
wrapped up in emotion as well
However, consider this ... if there was no crucifixion,
would you really believe that there is a Hell?

Position players do their jobs, so
we honestly must thank them dearly
because had they not fulfilled their purpose, as well
as they had,
would there be a "you and me"?
would "us" exists ... or would we simply remain a
fantasy?
Their inabilities may have appeared to have impeded
the journey
but access this time & space
Consider the hurricane

...

Let the winds blow as the rain helps heal the pain

and properly put things in place
US, discovered a natural formation
in our Garden of Serenity
This, is the union Yahweh has presented "we"
You pass thru me in a manner that I can best
describe as
phenomenally
unquestionably
unparalleled
by
Pleasure's Measure
Reminiscent of the first time my ears were
blessed beyond bliss by pleasantries offered from a
patient pianist who gracefully & tastefully
allowed keys to dangle from his fingertips
Pushing past the point of no return,
I am forced to forget that regrets
are afterthoughts
Compelled to tell those that care ...
tomorrow is a dream deemed needed by those
lonely souls who are not pleased today

Dare I say, if tomorrow never comes,
you have set my soul free
I do not wish to give you the world
I don't
I seek to lay the world at your feet, so you can

pick and choose what you want
I embellish the thought of you
and
I can comfortably unequivocally offer
you complete me

Dear

she was black
she was blue
she was brown

she was beautiful
she was beaten
she was broken

she was brilliant

like a jaded diamond with a royal cut,
she too could be called princess

ordaining years of love
enduring years of pain
spawning years of gain

she was and will always be,
my definition of what a woman is to be
she is
Dear

Descension

A touch ... a tease of a gentle breeze

No time for mistakes,
and less time for apologies
compromises are not on the agenda
and
excuses are a thing of the past

Looking at the world in motion,
my eyes are forced to
examine my surroundings
I see things now that I have
not seen in many seasons

Mindless ... Soulless ... Heartless ...
I am less the man I grew to know
Where is my instruction?
Where is my faith?
Where is my love?
Where are the elements that make me
ME?

What wisdom have I gained?
What mountains have I moved?
What heart have I cherished?

I am able to see Beauty …
naked & sincere
I am able to see my blessings …
prepared & honest
I am able to see Love …
pure & simple

Gracelessly,
I fall like a sparrow with two
broken wings,
wondering where the ground is
How far am I from the sea?

Cherishing Spring's break but
longing for Fall's end,
I'm wondering …
When will the madness cease?

Embellish a Breath

She
stood somewhere in the kitchen
at the corner of frustration & depression
He
sat at the table staring
at an empty paper plate food had yet to grace
Tonight,
there would be no mouth watering
scents dancing in the den
nor floating to the foyer
If anything was going to be served,
a heaping helping of white noise awaited

This, is where they were and no amount of
candid congenialities was about to change it
To be honest, she was relieved when all he did was
sit
up … down … it really didn't matter,
because at least he was able to remain in her
presence
She knew he was under pressure,

perhaps that is why she pressed
so ... extensively ... so, that ultimately ... he would
blow over & out

She simply stood there
She simply stood there awaiting an answer as he sat
staring at the empty paper plate no food would grace
It would appear as though the heaviest eyes on earth
resided at 616 Denial Drive,
as the strength of Sampson was needed to lift them
With his head ascended and his eyes & arms lifted ...
a fly could be heard hunting for food
A new sound entered the room as his throat cleared
And he began with:

I have been living life in a hair line fracture in Hope's
hip
I appreciate the opportunity and I invite you to listen
to my 'apology'
Yet, there isn't a damn thing I have done for me to
feel sorry
However, my defense must be presented properly
I
I have tried to answer that question a thousand and
ten times ...
and no suitable reply satisfied ... until now

If there is anything I am ashamed of, that would be it
... it appears to me that I am obsessed & a few
sandwiches short of a picnic because I ...
yes dear
there are a few things that I must admit
Phillips or Flathead because this is screwy,
but I'm believing that its better it's happening this
way ...
so, that maybe you can digest the severity of the
answer I am attempting to display

You know
every bump on your body been mapped
and
every crevice covered created a crater of creativity
so, I know what will please
I can make a marvelous melody of your shadow's
shadows body
making me choke on cheap air
not from your requisitioned necessity for me,
but because the cheap vision my mind imprisoned
sets into motion an ocean of obscenities
that remind me you are not there
You see, when I rose this morning, I reached for you
and I want so desperately to retain the thought
that needing me too, you opened & extended
yourself for me

merely that I may breath you
I have been addicted for some time
and I stand accused when I don't inhale
And well ... yeah ... while I'm being honest ...
was it as good for you as it was for me?
Last night, a tootsie roll would have been
swoll when it considers how well your tongue worked
overtime
Last night, the various words you spake,
spoke only 3 to me escalating
louder & louder ...
and would not hush ... especially as I attempted to
disregard it all
while I used your thighs as ear muffs
Last night, a peculiar moan echoed in my head
as we made love from dusk till dawn while
falsetto pitched tones fail from your lips ...
your hips sang & danced a song I had not heard in oh
so long
Last night ... I wish you were there
but, was it at least good for you?

Perhaps I am just a bit far gone,
but considering my body and your body
calls the apex where they collide, home ...
there is nothing natural about my laying alone

So, when I rose, I reached for you
just ... lie to me ... appease my vanity ... tell me that
you opened & extended yourself just so that I may
embellish a breath of you

Hence, I have tried to answer that question
a thousand and ten times too
and
perhaps a satisfying reply is all I have ever needed
The knowledge of why I love you,
rests with the understanding that I am never
complete
when I am without my air
How can I breathe without my fair share of ... you
So, yes dear, when I say "I just do", know
every letter condenses unseen sweat & tears that
secrete for you
every minute spent apart from you sends my
nervous system into shock, only to yearn for you
every time I close my eyes, I see the
beauty of the two becoming one with you
Thus, if "I just do" doesn't work for you, then please
accept
I cannot breathe without you

just ... lie to me ... appease my vanity ...
may I embellish a breath of you?

Ever Change

All he ever wanted was a dollar,
    but all he ever got was change …
The dangling things in peoples
      Possessions that they could do
  without
Not like he deserved any of it,
    but nonetheless … he got it

Was it service that made men's
  pockets bleed like a turnip?
Was it pity that made women
  clutch their accessories?
Was it charity that made children
  laugh at him?

All he ever wanted was a dollar,
    but all he ever got was change …
Bleeding tears like rain fall off of
  his nose … it's warming up again
    Spring … but he wonders …
    "Why must I feel fall?"

With eyes rolling in his head,
His mind fades to youthful
Dreams of a submissive future
But that future, yields to the
painful present of dying hope

a hope of something
a hope of everything
a hope of nothing

All he ever wanted was a dollar,
but all he ever got was change ...
The lint from your pocket will do

Fairy Tales

I lost my faith in fairy tales,
when the princess died in my arms
The never-ending story of bliss
had a major tragic flaw
compelled by passion
and
greeted with fear
no song should be sung by
a mistress in a veil

She sat in silence consumed
by the darkness that was her life
And when the sight of tomorrow left her,
she was overwhelmed by grief and strife
No knight could save this maiden
who was sinking in her soul
The dark matter that is the night
only hailed to the glare in her eyes

I offered penance in the expression

of my life to soothe her aching heart,
but the bed she made was occupied by another
And when she laid there, fading from the faith
that I could aid her, it was then I
noticed Death beside her

No amount of desire would pry her from
her lover, and no action of my own could assist
The never-ending story of bliss had reached
its peak ... her eyes drew back
and the sensual sound that fail from her
lips, was nothing more than a subtle sigh

Compelled by passion
and
Greeted with fear
She took solace in knowing that
Death was near
no song should be sung by
a mistress in a veil
I have lost my faith in fairy tales

finally

I have made many mistakes seeking that ...
that perfect kiss
Looking for the perfect mate will
always be a miss
(and truth be told the perfect mate
doesn't exist, but see I am simply searching for
someone perfect for me)

And like a southern sky that is
no longer disturbed by storms,
your smile is a welcomed sight
that detours all of my harms
Your kiss is as if Heaven has been
condensed ... no longer a part of the great hereafter,
yet placed on your lips
And like a summer soft song
performed by the flames
of an open winter's fire,
you make my soul smile
You are a majestic melody
You are a grand symphony

You are the sweetest silhouette
Heaven has ever known
Simply, you are beautiful

Loving you is easy, because I have been in love
with you from the moment I saw you
You have designed my dreams in a manner that
makes Desire demanding
And if I have but only one dream for the rest of this
life ...
I pray it remains you
You are truly my fantasy come true

Periodically, I wish that I were living my
next life at home alone
awaiting the arrival of my wife,
so that when you walked In it would
confirm my suspicion ...
that eternity is to be endured with you
I long to lay silently enveloped by your shadow
and encompassed by your smile
guided by the hope that my eyes
can taste the grace of your love

The more I see you, I seek to touch you
The more I touch you, I long to kiss you
The more I kiss you, I am lost in US

and US feels good

Not that I recall ever being lost, although I am certain
I was …
but I was never aware
But dare I say I wanted you yesterday …
and the day before that …
and the day before that …
and the day before that …
I wanted you the day before the day I met you,
and our chance meeting can be considered fate
That date, which is embedded in my mind,
should not be forgotten nor lost to time,
lest we forget

Yet, it should remain with us to show us that
US was always written in Destiny's scroll
And as we grow old, the days before the day we did
serves as the high cost of my being lost
The day we did should always resound as the
moments of love
in which your eyes supplied my guiding light
to lead this lost soul to a home that
I found in you

First Move

by
Kàllisto

Mind stimulation
Daily dialogue
Young pupil with eyes wide shut
Except with this
You have my undivided attention
Taking everything
As if it were vital information
Teach me.
Mind boggling – my move?
Challenge me.
Predator vs. prey scenario. Who's who?
Both pondering whether or not to
Pursue.
Flee or stay?
Retreat or let myself be taken?
Fallacious? No
Intrigued? Definitely
Curious – yet cautious, for fear of... of...
Of what?

Pleasure?
Defeat?
No, detection.
Wondering, waiting, watching, wishing,
Waiting.
Brain insisting walking away with feet
Refusing to follow commands.
Play by the rules ...
But were they not made to be broken?
Longing, languishing, yet learning still.
In the process ...
Contemplating, hesitating, re-evaluating ...
Finally reacting.
Queen pond up two.
Right knight in.
Twenty more moves.
Check your mate.
Or better yet – your King stands alone.
30 moves – no capture
Stalemate – we both win.
Purposely?
Possibly? Yet ...
Óuna preguntas aquí papí!
(One question here papi!)
who's white?

the Garden of Confusion

How many messages have I left

with your nursemaid that went

unanswered?

How many more must I leave?

Why can't you answer my call?

filling the void...

finding an excuse to hear your voice ...

do you hear me?

you don't even think of me,

your heart just blows ill winds

when compassion is the key,

how can you utter that you think of me?

if you are not needing me, then

why am I missing you?

in my distressed situation,

i find I need you more

in your time of need,

is it me you look to

or

the role I represent?

When simple submissions are

taken for granted,

what are one word replies?

What this feels like,

is nothing it was intended to be

But...

one day,

I am going to be wrong,

and the faith I have in you

will be shattered

It is only fitting ...

considering the circumstances of our love,

our lives are revolving doors

where the entrances that once were ...

come back around ...

what will be so much different then,

than what was?

the attitude is insane

and

the arguments are mundane

and you believe this is the beauty of charity

what wreaks the essence of Love?

love should not have to hurt,

to feel good

all things considered and questioned ...

these are the seeds you have planted in this

garden of confusion

Gone

Loose strings & broken buttons ...

with no seamstress in sight,

can the garment stay together?

Pieces and parcels of dreams pulled apart by

Pain

How together are we?

It seems that loose strings & broken buttons

are all we own

We have been trapped in the

wilderness to wonder

but you ...

you have been feeding me fruits of passion

From dead trees and withered vines

How then can you sacrifice your

First fruits from an ailing harvest?

What have we gained?

What have we learned?

What have we, except

a past?

Torture comes from the desire of

passionately wanting what is not there

I feel the dust settling though ...

the thought of what is lost,

haunts me to no end

but it is gone ...

losing something so precious

like a first born child,

I find my heart

soaking amidst a pool of

sorrow

good bye

Good Morning Love

Opening my eyes to a new day is not enough

This blessed event is overshadowed by an

even greater joy

The joy of bearing witness to the

beauty of you

So many nights have passed

with the beauty of you being

a figment of distant thoughts,

that this hardly seems to be true ...

But yet it is, because with every

passing blessed new day

I bear witness to the beauty of you

If that I were blind and could

not see this apparition anew,

I still would thank God for the

beauty in you

And I am grateful for each new day

that you see the same splendor as I do

So, as I dance in the rays of the sun and

sit in the shade,

good morning love ... and thank you for this

blessed new day

Grave Song

I feel so violated
I have been raped,
And no one seems to care!
Like a bad illusion,
It all happened too fast
But not fast enough for me not
To remember
My innocence has been robbed
Lost are the misconceptions
That life is what you make it,
And love is all you need
Love is a myth ...
A fairytale you tell your
Daughters to put them to bed
A song you sing to
Ease your mind during trying times
A legend that
Offers the hero a valiant reward
And life ...
Let's just say it was!
What is that sound?

Oh yeah,
Here come the knives!
Who in Hell ordered the execution?
I'm bleeding now
Reaper,
Why must you toy with me like this?
I was told that my death was to be
Quick and Painless
I guess Death lied about that too!
No matter ...
I've lost the desire to try
I've drowned my will
I'm not sure if it was your happiness
Or
You not loving me that drove
Me insane
I know I'm gone now!
Funny though ...
Of all the demeaning moments
In my life, I've never felt more
Worthless in all my days
Nonetheless, you are happy ... right?

Here & Now

A thousand thoughts per second

A million problems per minute

One resolution per hour

All for

A moment of peace

Color defines time

Time dictates emotion

Emotion designs color

My imagination has stolen

The best of me

An overlapping continuum that

Has no breaking point

How did it all begin?

One step away from Heaven

And

Half an inch from Hell

This hurts ...

Knowing I am so close, yet

feeling so far away

I do not desire to detour to my

Prior position ...

Nor am I looking forward to my

Distant disorder

The here and now ...

That's what matters in the end

When does the sorrow cease?

insanity's Silence

If I could feel my feet beneath me,
then perhaps I could stand
But my faith has become like an old worn rag
that I hope holds in my hands

The agony of ignorance has me stupefied
as I consider the number of
blessed dress rehearsals
when I should have died

Yet
I admit
I have an addiction
but all that I ask,
Is that you listen
My definition of beautiful,
says we met somewhere betwixt & between
over the counter and thru the woods
To something euphoric I know
where we sit and sing on angels wings
laughing at the flight of purple snow

My dear don't you know,
we have a majestic love mission

Yet
I sit
I sit waiting for the phone to ring
I sit waiting for my heart to sing
A half lit cigarette serves as testament
that time has been spent
that reality has been bent
I am dancing down that fine line that
separates the sane from those that have not,
and I have got seven minutes to sunrise to
make a play in this plot

It is the waiting that bothers you the best
Time seems to take a detour at the front door,
while Despair keeps you company
Hurry up and wait, is the mode of operation in play
the plan of the day
Albeit, a slow sensual burn on Satan's stove
is what gravely awaits
Why should you flirt with Desire,
when Destruction takes your hand?
And when dreams no longer saves your sinking soul,
Destiny itself grabs you by the throat and takes
control

Contaminated blessings flow from windows that
remain closed
...
a cruel & cheap illusion presented by Delirium, when
Summer winds blow cold
Ultimately, yet ironically, it is Death,
that knows you the most

Yet
I admit
I have an addiction
and all that I ask,
is that you listen
My definition of beautiful,
says we met somewhere betwixt & between
over the counter and thru the woods
to something euphoric I know
Where we sit and sing on angels wings
laughing at the flight of purple snow
My dear don't you know,
we have a majestic love mission

You see
this morning,
I woke up
I woke up from a black & white dream that
offered me no color

only hazy shades of gray
I woke up from hues of concepts rooted in fantasy,
when all that I needed
was realism
All that I needed, was something to serve as evident
evidence
that my living, had meaning
that my breathing, did more than poison the
midnight air
that there was some grand scheme that I served,
and my suffering would someway one day lead to my
salvation
However,
this morning, I woke up drowning in a depression
while featured in a dream I was not dreaming
questioning my suffocating soul that keeps sinking
...
is my breath worth breathing
does my blood merit bleeding
is my heart worth beating
?

I admit
I have an addiction
all that I ask,
is that you listen
I sit in a dimly lit room,

wanting desperately to end it all
A full lit cigarette serves as testament
that time has been spent
that reality has been bent
that this cyclic redundancy of severe stupidity
needs a ready replacement
that my name should be a marvelous melody in your
mind,
as opposed to fragmented figments of fallacies
that do nothing more than waste time
Honestly, I feel like an artists tag attached to some
mundane mural sprayed on just another brick in your
wall
Yet, I sit in silence in a dimly lit room,
waiting for the phone to ring
when will you call?

it's ok

I stood in front of the dead-end sign next to the
house,
on my heels
rocking back & forth ... arms stretched out
wishing I had wheels
I shot off down the street, fast as I could
lifted my head, opened my eyes
and I began to glide
positioned myself properly,
and I began to fly
my perspective altered, if but for a brief moment in
time
never really mattered that these innocent
images rested in my dying mind
I was higher than I had ever been, and it was all so
surreal
just like an illusion ... something short of a dream
even still, flew too high and singed my soul
leaving what returned with putrid black wings
However,
mines was never to dine with hypocrites

or
dance with demons from the past
serve society as love's martyr
or
keep my heart's flag at half-mast
mines, was the hope that you could never grasp
mines, was the belief that we would somehow make
love last
now, dreams are things Faith tells me I cannot trust,
although I must
I have never been an advocate of suicide ... never
been my forte
so, when she reaches for your hand dear,
understand ... sweetheart
it is OK

These things called wings do get heavy to hold,
although when ill-winds do blow,
I am never too cantankerously cold
While we were together, the weather never did
let up to allow us to catch up with one another
We were never riding the same thermal to overstand
each other ...
no wonder why my neck hurts, looking for love in the
sky
I, was never designed to fly this low
some seasons can only last for so long

So, long as I was here, why not give living a try
However,
mines was never to dine with hypocrites
or
dance with demons from the past
serve society as love's martyr
or
keep my heart's flag at half-mast
mines, was the hope that you could never grasp
mines, was the belief that we would somehow make
love last
now, dreams are things Faith tells me I cannot trust,
although I must
I have never been an advocate of suicide ... never
been my forte
so, when she reaches for your hand dear,
understand   sweetheart
it is OK

Many moons have past since my last flight where
even eagles would dare
I have seen several sunsets and added many more
regrets,
since those troublesome times I have attempted to
forget
those days since last that I cared
Spent several sleepless solitary nights

that I would have rather had shared
However, considering my life is an epitome for
passion,
when Peace presents herself, I would like to be
prepared
when "in love", I love hard
when I must let go, it is like I am AWOL
awaiting a dishonorable discharge

So, when Sanity said grab hold of Reality,
I realized that the hour to remain here is at its last
mines was never to dine with hypocrites
or
dance with demons from the past
serve society as love's martyr
or
keep my heart's staff at half-mast
mines, was the hope that you could never grasp
mines, was the belief that we would somehow make
love last
now, dreams are things Faith tells me I cannot trust,
although I must
I have never been an advocate of suicide
it has never been my forte
so, when she reaches for your hand dear,
understand ... sweetheart
it is OK

Karma Sutra

She wanted to know if I could make her scream my
name
I responded,
"If it's all just the same, I'd rather feed from your
femininity and sequentially appease my thirst
with sips from your soul" ...
be so bold and ask with me, would you
find pleasure in going home?
The acoustics are nicely designed
for soft subtle moans

Let's journey to Neptune
I'm sure you would enjoy my planet ...
many are not this privy
We can drink from Desire's well
as we partake in a hajj to the glorious Erotic City
travel uptown for a little D.M.S.R.
while my hands hunt a hidden treasure
Here, my dear, there are 189 different ways to
define the word pleasure

We could watch a play written by my aunt, Venus ...
then feast on Starfish & Coffee
We could play in the purple rain of Ra,
then mount the reigns of ecstasy
Lusting for one another is never a sin my sweet ...
it is a luxury
With a plethora of positions to choose,
how would you wish for this prelude to end?
Nothing is ever in excess,
since there is no limit to the joy to spin

We could spin a bamboo like lotus,
watching the 3rd moon roll back for the sun ...
We could act like crabs on a deserted shore,
while witnessing the legislation of a cow
While delighting in a blow from a boar
We can suspend Congress and witness
a woman at the helm
I can dim the candlelight's & raise the oceanic aroma
to heighten the ambience in this realm
You can pretend to be the wife of Indra
as I align our chakaras for retention
I'll be the Head of State as you transcribe
my dictation for comprehension
When words become insufficient,
we could simply hold each other as I
ascertain tomorrow in your eyes ...

While you conjure the name you seek to yell,
I'll seek shelter from Hell betwixt your thighs
And I, who was lost,
can now be claimed found inside you
Our harmony will be heard by the masses,
as we make one from two
And you, who was once found,
can now be claimed lost as we cross the 7 Black Seas

Tonight ... tonight and every night hereafter
do not refer to me as SocraTeez
During this and these,
our own Karma Sutra,
simply refer to me as
Dr. Please

Lost Sounds

I am hearing sounds of

underground trains,

where none exists ...

trampling over distant tracts

I am hearing sounds from

trees that speak,

where none exists ...

whispering directions to a labyrinth

I am hearing sounds of

grounded cherubs,

where none exists ...

wondering how they may

get their wings back

Precisely,

I am hearing things

I am hearing I love you

I am hearing things

I am hearing I want you

I am hearing things

I am hearing I need you

I am hearing things

I am losing my mind

I am out of control

love Song

broken and torn

bitter and touched

burdened and tart

  a rush of emotions

  a plague of feelings

  an undeniable notion

    Delirium standing before you

    Desire seated behind you

     and

    Death knocking at your door

    can you hear Love calling?

    has it ever felt like this?

the Mirage

Laying low and keeping still
Watching her every move
She saw me once and I saw a luster in her eye
I examined every curve on her body
I caught every tone of her flesh
I discovered every thought on her mind
But now, her back is turned
and she thinks I went away
But I am here ...
In the calm of the brush ...
feeling the breeze ...
catching her scent
She wants me
She knows I am after her,
but she doesn't know when I'm going to take her
I'm going to have her ...
She wants me to
But this is a game
A game I have already won
I just need to claim my prize

I bolt from the brush
while her guard is down
Catching her from behind,
she squirms for false freedom
Fighting will do no good
I seized your mind moons ago
Your body is all I need to make this complete
Crawling up your legs,
I long to taste everything you are
Gracefully hovering my tongue
over the creases of your skin,
you appear to cease the thought of sparring
My hands can not help but notice
the softness of your skin
The curves my eyes had only admired,
my hands are delicately embracing
Bathing her in my delight
her head tilts back ...
her back arches ...

I hear her moan sweet surrender,
but she wants more
This calms you down,
but is it enough?
What more do I have to give?
Yes ...

She wants me to give her all of me
Will she be satisfied with that?
Is my head enough,
or does she want my soul too?
Yes ...
She wants my soul as well
I see that now
She screams in ecstasy
Yes ...
The pleasure I present
You can not do this alone

I have won
She let me
She wanted me to win
Sipping on the solution she wishes me to have,
I think of nights I have dreamed of this moment
And I will gladly go through it
all over again to have a taste
of the delectation she is giving me now
I would suffer through this
game to drink from your cup
This elation is no illusion
Squeezing my very spirits from me,
you show an ounce of fear
Don't be afraid
This is only the beginning of this

love affair
As you notice ...
The hands have been dealt
The game has been played
The courtship is over
This is no longer a mirage

Morning Oath

Dreams, like glass goblets, are fragile yet firm
They sit on shelves waiting to be dusted
They become centerpieces for show,
if ever anyone wanted to look at them
We share them with our friends
from time to time
We drink ... We make merry, and
we have a feast with them
And when the party is over
and the others are long gone,
we festively toss them around
to place them back on the shelf
But I ... I am both
Convinced and Committed
I am convinced that my
dreams are achievable
And
I am committed to
see them through
To give up now, would be a sin
There are too many people to please, and

someone will be left disgruntled

       The cemetery is perhaps
      the richest place on earth
Not because of the bodies that inhabit it, but because
      of the thousands of dreams that are
        buried in it
    Would it be better to take from me,
    that which I did not give myself?
    If I looked at everything once more,
    would I see anything unusual?
    Wanting to hold on until the end,
    I summon every seed of solace
    I have in me
Fearing the unknown and weary of the uncertain, my
mind is content to stay
where I am... but my soul siphons more
The cesspool that has drowned dreams before,
will not possess mine
    For the future offers endless possibilities
    It is a web yet to be weaved ...
    and only the spider who spins it
    knows what He is doing
    Why should I give up and give in
    to that which has not come to pass?
Press on
 That's what my soul says ...
  Press on

Muted Man Memoirs

I stood at the edge of Desire
staring into an abyss of emotions
that have left me numb
from an overflow of sentimentality
that defies all practically
I have motionlessly awaited a sign
flyin' high into the sky like a
rocket man, traveling in whatever
direction the wind
North, East, West ... however, South
seems to inevitably be the course of which
I am damned
Have you heard the news?
We suffer from an endless saga of
uninterrupted inner city blues
So, why are we so green?
I mean, why are we so confused
regarding our purpose ... our goals?
Why do we accept this sordid reality
while having these sadistic dreams?
Why are we so quick to trip on our own,

knowing the same place they lay their head
is where we call home?

Hell, we misuse, abuse, rape & rob
from people in our own hoods ...
So, why should we look to others who don't give
2 shits about "us" to do us some damn good?
Using food for thought and thought for food ...
chew on this

As sickening as it sounds,
many of us aren't that much different ...
Kelly just let a tape rape his ass, but we are
just as sick in every single way
Hell, we piss on other people around us every day

We belittle, demean & degrade each other
like it aint shit ... speaking of which,
it's only a matter of time before some
pop black icon self records his sexually frustrated ass
tryin' 2 get erect with some poor child
while having a bile movement
3 days later, human pop fecies will be
floating on the net for the whole world 2 see
I wonder ...
how many of us will believe them when we see them
on the 6 o'clock news and they have the gall to utter,

"Yeah that's my crib, but that shit aint me!"

Time 2 tweak the truth

The youth are an adequate display for a lacking of
common knowledge and understanding
as a result of perplexed parental parody
They are classically conditioned to mimic the
idiotacy,
of which in their own homes everyday, they see
No man can teach a girl how 2 be a woman, like
no woman can teach a boy 2 be a man
The notion that that is possible is as
asinine a man with 2 amputated arms saying,
"Say brotha, I need another hand."

Echoes of what any child will become,
can be found in their homes
Mama and/or daddy used 2 train children
in the ways they should go ...
hell, these, days, we pop'em an allowance,
an X-Box and/or a PlayStation, BET/MTV
and hand them a damn cell phone
It's real cute Kiki knows the latest dances
she drops it like it's hot, scrubs the ground,
then shakes it like a salt shaker for everybody 2 see

However, don't grab a leather belt when she walks up
and says,
"All I want for X-Mas is a pole mommy" ...
because Kiki aint but 3
Women continuously blaming sorry ass runaway men,
while
men blaming hoeish naggin' ass women ...
it's the same old song
When will we finally face the fact that some shit is
just
DEAD ASS WRONG!

2 much emphasis is being placed on "head of
household" status
and
we are at a loss as 2 how 2 make families work
There are 2 many women tryin' to wear a pair of
pants,
and at the same time
there are 2 many men tryin' 2 wear skirts

Unity says $1 + 1 = 1$, truly now that's what it do!
So, what do we do while running from thorns in
bushes
sinking in stupidity's
cesspool?

Do we search for solutions
and offer alternative answers
to the existent ignorance,
or do we simply continue to
overlook our present degradation,
seek 2 outshine & outbling each other ...
all the while playing the
world's fool?

Honestly people, what do we do?

the Naked Eye

Simmering emotions that burn like
coals in a winter's fire
Looking for Love in a dancing flame
Blinded by colors that the naked eye
should not see, where can
Love be found?
Is it in the heart of the fire?
A drunken notion can lead one to
think that all is well
But when broken illusions are all that
are possessed,
charity is a fleeting memory
Loosed to the idea that
forgiveness can offer a remedy, where can
Love be found?
Is it in the dissolution of a damaged eye?

Nonetheless

Whether or not we actually accomplish anything at
all,
  We have accepted fate
Though it may not be our intention to plague our
minds with
  pretentious fallacies or maligned incongruities,
    We are nonetheless off
How have our heads fallen so low?
How have we fallen so short?
How have we fallen?
Is fate an acceptable wheel to be driven,
  or is it a road to be traveled?
Whatever it may be called,
  let it never be called friend of ours!

We, who have aimlessly traveled through the night ...

  Searching for the unburied tomb

  Searching for the seventeenth wonder

  Searching for the ladder that Jacob built

Why?

Why have we?

Why have we fallen?

Is this the accepted journey of a lost people,

  or is this the ride of a misinformed nation?

Whether or not we actually accomplish anything at

  all,

    we have accepted fate

Though it may not be our intention to plague our

  minds with

    pretentious fallacies or maligned incongruities,

    We are nonetheless off

Aren't we???

on the Road to Kashmir

rested remaining restless
recurring themes in my dreams
that deem me less than blessed
Why have I traveled a thousand tears,
only to cry for Death?
removed of every ounce of pride
and
devoid of the last liter of right I had left
I am a fool by nature
and
frustration has found me at every turn
Although 3 lefts may make me right,
the fourth detours me in the same
destructive direction I was going
down
...
damn
A pastime paradise mutes my mind
Death be so kind as to dine at my table tonight,
because breathing is for the birds
I heard

...
sight, is a useful function for those that cannot hear
...
feeling, is a fortune when the lethargic lends an ear

I am in desperate need of a suitable substitute
for serenity
Sanity, let me go long ago
And although I know her replacement
can hardly be considered comparable,
dare I say Despair keeps me plenty company
When sane meets insanity,
even the dysfunctional can appear promising
Concrete ash kept my mind tied to
dreams that floated among the debris
that ignorance afforded me
And I ... I who would lie with the lions,
would never be pardoned for my losses
lost time
lost thoughts
lost loves
Black doves fly five thousand miles,
only to dive and die at my feet
Fortune, would never be my friend
I have greeted Despair with a loving smile,
all the while hoping for Death to
remove me from my delirium

Yet, I would dream of concrete ash
that would keep my desires tied to
a horse that would never die
And I
found my hands buried
beneath the desert sands

rested remaining restless
my immoral morality keeps me carnal
accustomed to the darkness
and creeping things in the corners of my mind
afraid of the shadows I do not see
and the torrential rain pain brings
adhering to my hunger and enlightened carnal
cravings
and seeking only illusions in the end
Repeated past gestures of loathsome delights
that the night dares to see
Why does my heart, then, entertain
such an obscure confederacy?
Why does my soul dance
with demons and derelicts?
Why does my mind wane,
when wonders are beyond visible prospects?
Fleeting thoughts and flowing dreams
In but a moments passing, have I seen such things

Thoughts as swift as the wind and dreams as evident
as the air
Why must it be so complicated to catch a whisper in
the wind?
Security is for the weak and uncertainty for the
confused
Is there then a gray
where the fear feeds fortune?
I pray it ends promptly,
while my eyes are accustomed to my misery

rested remaining restless
on the road to Kashmir

out to Sea

There is a man who lives by the sea
He dwells in an old wooden home
with his dog and the dust
As the breeze blows in, the
sea speaks ever so calmly to him
Ever so gently does the midst from
the sea winnow in,
touching his heart ... tickling his soul ...
reminding him of drowned dreams

One such dream had not sank,
but was barely treading water
At about the time the glory of the
day had reached its peak,
a tardy tide was pushing
the perishing dream to shore

The man saw his phantasm,
and retrieved it with passion
Being satisfied with nothing for
so long, he decided to

build a ship and set sail with
his dog and his dream

Many people saw him
and thought he was restoring
his home
But when the figure resembled a boat,
his admirers quickly became
deriders
Those that at one time
cherished his craftsmanship,
now thought of him as foolish
Even his best friend barked
at his efforts
It is one thing to be mocked by others,
but when your own begin
to ridicule you ...
Hope and Delirium
are all you have left
Which would you choose?

The man chose Hope
as his new companion
He and Hope were to
complete the ship
on their own
Those that returned to examine

the mockery, were
amazed at the final results ...
not only did the boat float,
But He, Hope, the dream, and
the boat had set sail

Stunned and baffled,
they noticed a note on
the front door of the broken home
As they approached the
door, the letter
became more legible

It read:
"To those of concern and
those of criticism,
I have opened my main sail and
I am riding the waters of life
Is my labor still humorous?
Is my mission still vague?
Is the sagacity still sound?
I would surmise that at this point,
my efforts are finally clear ...
I am off with Hope to
revive a dream
Look for me no longer ...
I am OUT TO SEA"

the Perfect Storm

I'm a freak from Neptune
wanting to eclipse your moon soon
Play with your lunar objects that
perplex my scene while you
encompass my being
Even when I dream you are there
Stars stop and stare at the glare
of our celestial team
I simply want to be to you
what you are to me
Appreciated to the point you are
elevated but still within reach
Admired and adored
to the extent that gravity is bent
Floating on natural gasses
while meteors pass us
Under the indigo night
everything seems right
You in front of me
Me behind you
This is the perfect moment to

ask… can I kiss you?
You see, it's the nearness of you
It's the voodoo that you do
so damn well
I can tell that those deeds
of dreams and fantasies fulfilled
are meant for me
And be that as it may
we vary in form,
we merge like two winds
and create a storm
Floating on natural gases
while meteors pass us,
our geographical positions
provide the essence for the
perfect storm
With pressure rising
amidst this black moon's
horizon, there is no safe haven
nor time for compromising
However, you see for me, there's no
safer place on Earth
than being between two thick thighs
And yours look just right
for my appetite
Don't let the size fool you,
I do own the tools to woo you

once we
set the
merger into motion
"I can picture us creating rain
and from the lovin' we'll spark a flame
oh I love it, cuz you see the same
and when the day breaks we'll do it again"
Like an old Chaka Kahn tune, let's do
that there
so we can do it again
Float... Float... Floating on natural gases
while fragments of meteors pass us
The barometric pressure is rising
as my cirrus meets your stratus
and we make a
cumulo – cirro – stratus...
a nimbus
some rain clouds
to drench this scene
to make multiple wet dreams
for this... this perfect storm

Pink Elephants Walk

A slipknot called seduction
grabs me by the neck and drags me
33 feet
Tossing me 720 degrees
from nowhere
sending me anywhere, accepting the
knowledge I cannot be
everywhere
My limited scope allows me to
concentrate on pieces & participles
small tidbits of ecstasy are ...
are present day illusions succumb
to harsh realities of neglect and suppression
Like a stigmatic on an inverted cross ...
Pleasure? No!
Pain? Infallibly ... YES!
My life is an etcha-sketch ...
translucent drawing that has become
shaken & stirred
No absolute sight, my vision
is blurred

No circumference circle, straight
lines occurred
No perfection, rough ashlars
spurred
If this is my fate, then let me
deteriorate because a soulless
existence can hardly be defined
as living
And if my cross wards one from
danger, then my tears are
not in vain
If my life is but a grain
of sand in a forgotten and lost land,
then great expectations tell
tales of a great depression
So, what is expected but
lost illusions and grandiose delusions
that offer pain at a buried
alter?
Why am I on knees?

Plea Bargain

How can you abandon a
love that has already
tried our transgressions?
How could we be found guilty?
(although you say that we are)

Let us not look at the things we have
done,
and allow those things to
dictate what we can achieve

I am puzzled …
when I needed you the most,
you thought it better for you to depart
But what about us?
What about me?
What happened to being there for the
One you love?
Something just said?
Something just read?
Something just done!

Was it a tale told in the
voice of passion?
or
was it a promise passed in the
flight of the foolish?
It takes two to make a fool
One to be the fool
and the
other to listen
Passion speaks to the fool
who is willing to
listen

Tell me you want me ...
to hear your voice utter those words,
would make my heart sing
Tell me you need me ...
gratification for me is too
simple for spoken words
Tell me you will please me ...
no matter how much I try to
dismiss the thought that you
do not crave me,
my heart can only envision that you do

But,
whatever you tell me ... do not tell me goodbye

there is nothing good about
bye

only painful pleas that bargain with
Betrayal

the Quest

Like an inverted cross in the desert ...
the red stains above a door from a sacred lamb ...
like a country's colors at half mast,
my hung low head is but a small symbol that
I am allowing Despair passage
I am allowing Desire to pass
I am no longer looking for one who
embodies all that I have ever dreamed of
I am no longer searching for access to my soul ...
one who fills in the voids and allows me the
opportunity to feel whole

I have become a visionless visionary ...
an innocent child's mockery ...
a blind artist who's hands pass over the keys,
but incapable of perfecting my own marvelous
melodies
I am an unmoved writer on a desperate quest for a
muse
Although I have been blessed by fleeting thoughts of
fulfillment,

I am forced to make
isolation my inspiration
No matter how I choose to use this
muse made from madness,
I am always led to a misleading mirage of
satisfaction,
which directs me to sadness

Just when an opportunity appeared to pass my way,
night falls
darkness hinders my ability to move and I am
forced to view my remains on the following day
Therefore,
I am no longer looking for a lullaby from Love
or
merely someone to simply lay with ...
I am desperately seeking my muse
I am awaiting the one who I can say hello to the sun
and
enjoy the rest of my days with
I am on a quest for someone who can soothe my soul
at ease
One who makes me feel like a better man,
because loving her is loving the gift God gave me ...
Someone I can speak to Yahweh with
I am on a relentless pursuit of the promise of
prolonged pleasure

Someone who makes monogamy, not a tragedy, yet a
treasure
and
we are exalted because
I and She makes
US
I am desperately seeking my muse …
seemingly, I have sought this seductress
every waking moment of this life
and my quest now requires that she
serves as my heart's horizon …
as my soul's lift
I am searching for someone
I can feel comfortable dying with

Sea of fools

I am laying here thinking about
the first thing that
comes to mind
after the last
thought

Swimming past the
Sea of Iniquity,
I find no bank to
comfort me
I can only think of
better days

How many nights have I
been traveling,
only to find I am
no further from my point of origin ...
when I began?

Voices in my head
have confused my course

I am not sure where I am
supposed to be,
but I know it is not
here

Sometimes
it is better to listen to your own
Voice,
instead of the voices of
others

However,
when you camouflage a situation
to make it seem more than
it actually is, then
what you do Is extinguish
the possibilities of
what could have
been

I am tired of running,
but I cannot stay still
There are too many issues
in my ocean
for me to tread amongst a
Sea of Fools

Sinking

Captured in a maze

with a noose as my guide

no candle ... no torch ... no light

to aid me in my quest

Broadened sense of insecurity

Heightened notion of fear

Aware of nothing

Inhaling the pain

and all the pleasure that comes with it

Numb to emotion,

I swim in a pool of misery

The unabridged version of loneliness only

expands my scope of obscurity

Staring at potentials, possibilities and actualities,

there is no preserver in my foreseeable future

Being pulled by love,

I hope to reach the end ...

soon

I am blessed to drown here

in this barren body that consumes me

taking me under

making me wait

keeping me still

Six foot Circle

pink pedals that fall from the fountain of charity
  grope my mind and entreat my soul
Loose leaves that follow my every move
  changing my every step
Torn trees with no roots
  offer solace in shades of gray
Broken by surrender and anointed by despair,
  where is my heart to find grace?
I have searched since the beginning of time,
  and still I have yet to find my treatise
Overcome by belief and overwhelmed by bypasses in
the night,
  how do I continue to seek the unseen?
Why should I wonder about
  forgotten seasons and lost cities?
Why should I wonder about
  fading stars and loose causes?
Why should I wonder about
  missed opportunities and rushed actions?
Why should I wonder?

a light fixture with no chord
a burned-out bulb
a repeating record
a warped woofer
a tubeless television
a foiled antenna
an elevator with broken buttons
a lacerated heart with no veins
No light ... No sound ... No sight ... No might ...
forever planted on the ground
and I thought I had it bad,
  simply because I lost my life!
Then I begin to think ... about ...
pink pedals that fall from the fountain of charity
  grope my mind and entreat my soul
Loose leaves that follow my every move
  changing my every step
Torn trees with no roots
  offer solace in shades of gray

I observed her motions from a dark corner in a dimly
lit room
She possessed all the beauty of a queen
I had seen her kind, but only in my dreams
Yet, there she was
amidst the average
walking among the ordinary
residing among the mediocre
There she was
exhibiting every physical aspect I have ever yearned
And, there she was ...
overcome with curiosity
overtaken by mental stimulation
overwhelmed with obsession

She wanted to be a willing participant in pleasure
and she needed me to notice
She needed me to notice that for me,
her body would be my private island
I could travel her terrain
hike her hills

or
simply vacate in her valley
She needed me to notice that for me,
fantasies would be fulfilled
Destiny & Desire would not just exists in Dreams
She would reconstruct creation and let there be us
She would feed me hors d'oeuvres of ecstasy made of
her essence
as I drank from a well filled with her nectar
She needed me to notice that we would be gods,
if I could only see the same
We would make one from two
and her smile would erase all my pain

And as I entertained those thoughts, I asked
could I be the embodiment of Desire when you
dream?
And she, with evident elegance,
gracefully yet tastefully reframed from answering
She wanted to tell me yes
but something inside her said no,
because all she would ever do is want
All she would ever do is develop the desire,
but she would never see it thru
All she knew is what she had done
and

a myriad of movements that she swore she would
never do
again
She had allowed others to define her
and those definitions
(as confused as they were)
are the ruling bodies to what she is to become
nothing

She was/is afraid to get hurt
so, she simply waits
She waits for deception
but it will never come
With her eyes, she waits for the lies
but they will never come
With her heart, she would have to humble herself
but she never would

Before she stood to bless me, she left me
She left me sinking solemnly in an abyss
deeper than the depths depression
should allow one man to go
And I don't know whether it is the fact that
love is equivalent to pain and
she had already been down that path before
In me, she sees the Same Old Sewage
Perhaps, it is the belief that

all men are dogs and all we want is a bewitch and
since she had already won an Oscar for her last "Best
Bewitch Performance",
her next role would have to be a switch
Maybe it is simply ...
in order to give love, one must know what love is
and she has never been shown real love to
love herself with so ... she simply waits

She waits for words, when actions are unequaled
She waits for the sequel to a love song she has never
known
So, even if I told her how beautiful she truly is to me
told her how insatiable we really could be
showed her the fantasitical possibilities
would she even listen to me?
or
would she simply wait for another love song?

my sister ... my queen ... my dream
do not look too long with your hands in the sands
searching for pearls on the road side
let me dry your eyes
we shall discover the beauty that lies
inside
and
write a love song the world has yet to recognize

Sound

When I stare into your eyes,

I get weak with desire

Drowned by passion,

I am covered with red rose pedals

Uncompromised joy fills the air

and

Relentless pleasure consumes me

This is nothing new ...

You are my muse, and

You are my friend

You are my confident guiding light

You are my soul's half, and

You are my conscious

You are all that represents right

You are my lover for life,

even if we never make love again

Our love is already made

When yesterday ends

and

Tomorrow begins,

that is where we will be ...

riding on the wings of Hope

If God shines on us half as much as

We smile at each other,

We will be sound

Stairway to Heaven

Pt. 1

Traveling thru days of winter
Longing for moonlit escapades on
Italian shores
Crossing over Sahara sands
nearing your stairwell

In the midst of night
Summer's haze and Pale moon's light ...
an anchor has been cast
Thus, my journey begins

Viewing the glory before me,
time befriends me and I
know that Fate entrusts me ...
while Enchantment entreats me

As with all good things,
there are seven steps ...
there are five gates ...
there are three initiatives

The mere thought of you
creates a simmering desire,
which leads me to this action ...
I need you

On a cloud of silence and
a darkness that surpasses the night,
innocence is lost
With closed minds we have seen into
the limited fragments of our engagement ...
we have begun
Nothing is exactly the way it should be and
knowledge has not yet been known ...
we feel with our minds
intrigued by passion
and
persuaded by interest ...
that which we conceive, is

If you are a lullaby
and
I am a tune,
do we sing in the same key?
If you are a star
and
I am the sky,
does the world marvel at our beauty?

If you are wisdom
and
I am understanding,
do we complete knowledge?

Like a book, we are valued
only by what is within ...
not by the façade that
graces the cover

I have found you to be my heat
during days of winter
I have found you to be my peace
on pleasurable shores
I have found you to be my treasure
in a world of sifting sands

This is not Jacob's ladder,
but it is my stairway to Heaven
The closer I climb to you,
I am reminded of what Heaven on earth truly means

Love is not found in dreams,
but you are the essence of my imagination

Summer Solstice

Summer winds and winter rains
blow calmly in my mind ...
the rain beats the pain
of a love gone bad
from my aching heart

I am haunted by a
melody, but I do not know why
I look from a
distance
I see the cloud's tears
with mixed emotions,
the sky screams in torment
I feel his anguish
through the window's pain,
I see I am not alone

The ease of the symphony
that plays in my mind
puts my soul to rest ...
I am never to far

from the song, but I have
not heard its tune in four moons

If I never see you,
will you love me?
If I never feel you,
will you love me?
If I never taste you,
will you love me?

Since what should never have been
is, is it too late
to say yes?

Ummm.!!!

There is nothing worse
than a burning desire ...
an unsatisfied need ...
an uncontrollable hunger

With all the passion that
surrounds this meeting,
I hope that this feeling
is more than mutual

I have wanted to taste you
for so long, that
every second is savored ...
every minute is memorable

Choosing not to bite you,
but allow you to fall in my mouth ...
some things are better when
they fall in your mouth ...
that is when you know it's hot

But I cannot allow you to cool
I want you now,
while you are hot
and I am bothered

This is the time to please me
There ...
Spreading you apart
Licking you up
Sucking you down

With my lips dirty
and
my tongue dancing,
I am not ashamed to suck my fingers
I hope this is as good for you,
as you feel it delightful for me

Oh ... I apologize,
would you like a cookie too?

Valentine

With open arms
and
empty hands,
I come to you
wanting your touch ...
needing your feel

And if the stars were to fade
And darkness loomed,
the light from your eyes
would suffice
And if the world were to
lose its riches and famine flourished,
the warmth of your smile
would satisfy
And if all around me were to
drown in a sea of fools,
your outstretched arms
would save me from the illumed ignorance

Why must I be wanting,

when you possess all that
I need?
Deserving of you?
Never
Delighted by you?
Always
Desperate for you?
Always & Forever

How can I express my
gratitude for the mark
you have made on my life?
How can I exclaim my
reproach for the despair
I feel when you are not near?
How can I exhume my
love, so that you much notice
that I need you much more than the air I breathe?
How can I?

There is nothing I could
possess for your taking, that
would show you how I
need you by side
I cannot inhale, let alone exhale,
if you not with me

The best that I can do
is simply tell you …
I love You

Waters fall

A trail of tears traveled to my cheek
In a cheap attempt to justify their end
Their end?
A repugnant reality where dreams die to soon
due to a
loss of support
and
a lack of will

The desire left a long time ago
And the only thing that resides,
is a sordid shell of what used to be
what was and what sustains
presents evident evidence
that there has been a
drastic dramatic change

The only recourse that surrenders a
prominent contention, is intervention
Who shall save me and from what demise?

I have contrived thoughts of black ice paved with
white rose pedals that leave a dark blue hue

And you ...
you who once held in the
bosom of your blessings & grace, now savor the
sweet
taste of curses conjured from malice and waste
If faith is plagued by doubt,
then what remains of the levee of belief is a
disturbed drought
Nothing holds back the sea,
when the gift of sight is silenced

Empty is the heart
when Hope no longer exists
amidst a translucent life
Colorless love does not equate to happiness,
nor does the thought that
silence can cure communication

Pink pavements of purple reigns
reside amongst the ashes
I have chosen to let
my hands speak for me, because
my tongue has been made mute

Far too often, others
impose their ignorance on you
And due to a lack of competence,
we let them override our own
intelligence and drown from our
diminished confidence

My heaven quickly became
my hell
in the blink of an eye,
because I traded constant consonants
of mosaic muses
for maniacal mirages

So, if trust is to be re-birthed
from the debris made by insecurity,
then let the levee break from instability

And let the waters fall

When

sitting in the darkness

of the pale moon light,

cold dry air brushes against

my cheek and

a myriad of thoughts rush

through my head

the still calm night offers

consolation, where none exists

laying in the arms of

fallen angels,

i can no longer run from the known

interesting thing about

life is the uncertainty of the

next step

although a plan exists,

it is always subject

to change

Pleasure offers me a cup of

Delight, and I simply accept

out of gratitude

casual conversation passes the

complexity of time

unaware of the extent to which my

cup has suffered, she simply says...

say what you want...

just say when

Whole

I cannot lie,
for it was your body that
caught my eye
(whole)
Though your mind was soon to follow,
it was your body that I wanted to swallow
(whole)
And when we rode a unicorn
thru Kashmir fascinated by the
third ring of Neptune...
it was then that I noticed I want you
mind, body & soul
(whole)
With every attribute that a
black woman prostitutes,
I want to
make you
mine
From the first moments
of flirtation,
to the last seconds of elation

I am imagining an image
of love
are you?
Do you see the
same things I am feeling?
Or, have the constellations moved?
Is Orion still at Venus' feet...
latched onto her waist
with his firmly placed face
at her thighs?
Or is he simply holding her hand?
What you see is important to me,
because only after I firmly
understand where you are
with us
can I truly progress to be your man
I am fantasizing an image of love...
are you?
With the passivity that passion brings,
yes my dear...
I want to make your body sing
Indigo is the color of seduction
and Imperial is the taste of pleasure
Enchanted is the set mood
and I believe inertia is where
I want the feeling to be
So, let me suck on your

brown sugar baby
because I am envisioning us
during this wet scene
called a dream
I want to
make you
mine
I am imagining an image
of lust...
are you?

Acknowledgments

First and foremost, I would have to thank God for making this project possible! The inspiration that flows from me is but a testament to the talents that He has bestowed upon me. None of this would be remotely possible, had it not been for the words I have been blessed to put together.

(WHY do I feel like I'm at an awards show?)

Many people have contributed to the success of this project. It would be HIGHLY improper for me not to recognize many of those individuals, who's support has been unwavering in one form or the other. Kathie: I thank you for ALL that you have done! One day, I shall reciprocate the love. My parents: by way of finances or sales, you both have been a great help! Friends: you all don't know how much you have encouraged this work. Thanks for the EVERYTHING peeps. The poetic "crew": Cherokee, Imperial, Blu, Se7en, Lil' Azz Jazz, Spencer "the Maddrummer", Fialka, Bar None, Bird, Kontrast, Angie G., Tasha T, Chris, Jeannette, Lady Silke, Ms. Marie, "Big" John ... OK, it's one too many of you to name! But you KNOW what I say, let's just DO DA DAMN THANG! Chris & Moe,

Chelle D, Cass and the rest of my DFW Family ... Shugg & the Crew, Dreena & April @ Optima Designs (5110 Griggs Rd. booth 151B: you keep me looking good (sometimes very good ;-). Keep up the excellent work sister(s)! My other squares & stars who've shown the love, keep it coming. Dave & Don @ the Red Cat Jazz Café ... the fam & staff at The Shadow Bar ... you know I got MUCH love for ya'll! And er'e body else who be feelin' a brother, 'preciate it ALL!

Special people who are special for no reason at all to me ... it's a wonder why you're special, huh? Just know that I love you ALL, or at least hope to grow to LOVE ya! I'm ready for my train ride now!!!

www.ingramcontent.com/pod-product-compliance
Lightning Source LLC
Chambersburg PA
CBHW061147040426
42445CB00013B/1596